Selecting Investments for Your Retirement Account
Second Edition

Richard D. Glass, PhD, CEBS

Investment Horizons, Inc.
A Registered Investment Adviser
336 Fourth Avenue
Pittsburgh, PA 15222
(412)261-5510

Published by

Investment Horizons, Inc.
A Registered Investment Adviser
336 Fourth Avenue
Pittsburgh, PA 15222
(412)261-5510
Fax: (412)261-5932

Printed in the United States of America

ISBN: 0-9638029-1-7

I would like to express my thanks to Stan Marshall for his assistance in this endeavor.

Table of Contents

Why You Should Read This Guide

Although this book was written for participants in self-
directed retirement plans, the material covered will benefit
anyone facing investment decisions.

In contrast to the past, today's retirement plan participants
determine how their savings will be invested. For those of
you familiar with investing, taking control of your money
can be a welcomed opportunity, but for others, it's a scary
prospect.

While this guide is written primarily for those of you in the
latter category, it can also be a reference for the more
experienced investor. Although investing is often more of
an art than a science, there are historical relationships and
concepts which can help guide your investment decisions.
The aim of this guide is to give you a quick education in
these basics.

Unfortunately, most of us are too afraid of losing our
savings. We put our money into investments which have
historically done most poorly and ignore the best perform-
ers. We worry about temporary losses and forget that over
time, most of us will recoup these losses. This behavior is
illustrated by the following example.

Chart 1 shows the results of the strategies employed by five
imaginary investors. Each year, from 1960 through 1990,
these investors put $3000 into their accounts. Bob invested
all of his money in a money market fund. Valerie put hers
into a fund which invests only in five year government
notes. Evie picked funds which invest in large company

stocks. Dan, the most aggressive, chose a small company stock fund. Stan, feeling that he had no idea which investments would do well over the long haul, decided to put equal amounts in each investment category. Each year he put $750 into each of the funds his friends invested in.

Five Imaginary Investors

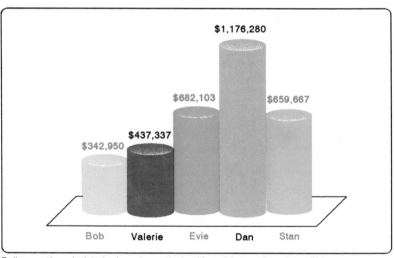

Dollar growths calculated using returns obtained from Ibbotson Associates, Chicago.

Chart 1

As you can see, Dan made the most money. However, he also had many a restless night as the value of his investments jumped up and down. Bob and Valerie slept best until retirement approached. Although their savings grew steadily, their accounts were relatively small compared to the others. Stan and Evie did about the same, but Stan's investments took much less of a roller coaster ride than Evie's. (The reasons are discussed later.)

These five investors were smart. They began saving at a young age. Unfortunately, many of us wait too long to begin investing for retirement. As shown in Chart 2, a 25 year old needs to invest only $25,400 to have $250,000 at retirement. A 55 year old, however, must invest $155,040 to reach the same goal. (For more on this, see page 12 and Appendix A. Monthly contributions are shown in Chart 21.)

The Price of Delay
(Savings Grow at 9% Until Age 65)

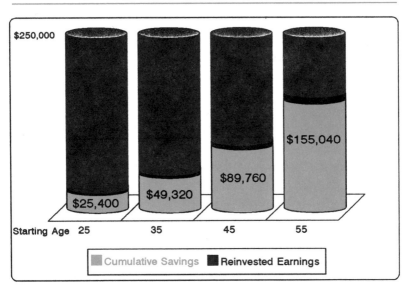

Chart 2

In the past, employers assumed the responsibility of investing money for their employees' retirement. Times have changed, however, and today, the responsibility of making investment decisions falls on your shoulders. Now you must understand the basics of investing to make intelligent decisions and provide yourself a secure retirement.

How This Guide is Organized

Although you can begin anywhere you want, starting with Chapter 1, Types of Investors, and then reading the section on returns, risk, and time (Chapter 2) is probably best. Chapter 2 explains the basics of investing and provides the framework for understanding the use of different types of securities (stocks and fixed-income).

Your retirement plan allows you to divide your money among several funds. (Funds are discussed in Chapter 5.) These funds invest in individual securities which are chosen by professional money managers. Since you invest in funds instead of individual securities, your employer has relieved you of much of the pressure of investing. On the other hand, the funds behave like the securities in which they invest. If stocks are riskier than bonds, then a stock fund is riskier than a bond fund. This is why we will spend time talking about individual securities. If you understand the way stocks and bonds work, then you can understand the behavior of stock and bond funds.

We also discuss how professional investment managers select securities so that you will have a better understanding of the descriptive materials you receive regarding your plan's investment options.

Successful investors have developed strong stomachs and the ability to sleep well when others are tossing and turning. Their confidence comes in large part from an understanding of past market performance, the role that time plays in investing, and the different types of risk.

Chapter 1: Types of Investors

What type of investor am I?

Traditionally, investors have been divided into two categories: conservative and aggressive. But now a third category is developing. Let's call them optimistic yet realistic (OYR). They are the ones who are educating themselves.

Conservative investors are preoccupied with the fear of losing money. They will give up the possibility of higher returns if there is even a slight chance of losing money.

Aggressive investors, on the other hand, know no fear. They are the gamblers of the investment world. They are willing to run high risks for the chance to hit the jackpot.

OYR investors try to find a middle ground between conservative and aggressive approaches. They want to earn relatively high returns, but they are not willing to take big gambles. They achieve their goals by diversification (spreading their money among several types of investments) and patience.

In the example in the section "Why You Should Read This Guide," Bob and Valerie are conservative investors. Evie is aggressive, and Dan is super-aggressive. Stan is an OYR investor.

There is no formula that provides a perfect strategy for investing your money. Whatever you do, however, don't lock yourself into a label on either end of the spectrum--conservative or aggressive. Use the information presented in this guide and the material provided about your plan's investment options to help guide your decisions. The better you understand the basics of investing, the greater are your chances of making money in the long run.

Chapter 2: Return, Risk, and Time

Investing is a marathon, not a 100 yard dash.
--Anonymous

Where do I start?

You must start by assuming that history will repeat itself. Over the long haul, stocks of small companies have outperformed those of larger companies, and both have done better than fixed-income investments. (See the chapters on equities [stocks] and fixed-income investments.) Unless we assume that the future will resemble the past, we have no basis for making decisions, and our investment choices will be made in an undisciplined, shoot-from-the-hip manner.

What are the basics of investing?

There are three basic concepts: return, risk, and time.

I've heard of returns, but what exactly are they?

Think of a return as how much money the investment earns during a specific time period, such as a year, quarter, or month. A return is usually expressed as a percentage of the amount invested. For example, if a $100 investment has a 10% annual return, in one year it will earn $10 and grow to $110. If it has a 10% monthly return, the investment will grow to $110 in one month and $314 in one year.

Returns can come in the form of cash payments, changes in an investment's value, or a combination of both. For example, if you put $100 in a savings account which earns 10% annual interest, your return is an interest payment of $10 (usually in cash). If you buy a house for $100,000, and a year later it's worth $110,000, you also earned a 10% annual return even though you did not receive a cash payment.

An investment's total return is the sum of all of its cash payments plus any changes in its value. The total return of stocks and bonds usually consists of both cash payments and changes in value.

Because returns can vary considerably from period to period, it is important to analyze returns during the same time period when comparing investments.

What is risk?

Risk is the chance that you will not achieve your investment goals.

Could you give examples of risk?

The simplest is losing money. When this happens, the investment is said to have a negative return. For example, if you buy a stock for $50 and, a year later, it's worth only $40, you lost $10 or 20%. Thus, the stock is said to have had a return of minus 20%.

Another risk is loss of buying power. Buying power--or purchasing power as it is often called--is a measure of the goods and services you are able to purchase. You lose buying power when your investments do not keep pace with inflation.

As you know, inflation drives up prices. Remember when candy bars cost a quarter? Today, however, you need 50 cents to buy one. Thus, 50 cents today has the same buying power that a quarter had in the past. If you had invested that quarter, and today that investment had grown to only 40 cents, you would have lost 20% of your buying power.

Are you saying that to maintain my buying power, an investment must earn at least the inflation rate?

That's right. If an investment's return is equal to the inflation rate, then you just break even. If it is higher than inflation, you come out ahead. But if the investment's return is less than the inflation rate, you've lost some buying power.

Besides returns and risks, are there any other important factors in investing?

Time is important in a number of ways. You must know how long it should take for an investment to obtain the desired rate of return. If one investment takes a year to return 10% and another takes two years, the first one is more attractive.

This is also where the idea of compound returns comes into play. To understand compound rates of return, we must first understand the differences between simple and compound interest.

With simple interest, interest is paid only on the original investment (the principal). For example, if you put $100 in an investment earning 10% annual simple interest, each year you get 10% of $100 or $10. (See Chart 3.)

With compound interest, on the other hand, interest is paid both on the principal and any earnings (interest) from previous years. If you put $100 in an investment with 10% annual compound interest, in the first year, you would earn 10% of $100 just as with simple interest. In the second year, however, you would earn 10% of $110 (principal plus first year's interest) or $11.

Chart 3 shows that your money grows faster with compound interest than simple interest.

Simple and Compound Interest

Year	10% Simple Interest		10% Compound Interest	
	Money Earned	Year End Value	Money Earned	Year End Value
1	$10 (10% of $100)	$110	$10 (10% of $100)	$110
2	$10 (10% of $100)	$120	$11 (10% of $110)	$121
3	$10 (10% of $100)	$130	$12 (10% of $121)	$133

Chart 3

In the above example, the annual interest rate did not change. The returns of many investments, however, change every year. To find out how an investment has performed over time, it is helpful to ignore the different annual returns and just ask: What constant compound interest rate would have caused the investment to grow as much as it did? This rate is called the investment's annual compound rate of return. It is this return that is usually shown in advertisements and sales materials.

Since the mathematics of compound returns can be difficult, their meaning can best be understood by example.

Assume investment A earns 10% compound interest each year for three years. If you put $100 in this investment, after three years it would be worth $133. (See Chart 4.)

Investment B, on the other hand, had a 20% return the first year, a negative 8% return the second, and a 21% return the third year. If you put $100 in this investment, it would also be worth $133 at the end of three years. Investment B, however, grew along a very different path than investment A. (See Chart 4.)

Since investment B grew as much over the three years as investment A (which actually earned a return of 10% each year), we say that investment B also had an annual compound rate of return of 10% for those three years regardless of its yo-yo like path.

Two Investments With a
10% Annualized Rate of Return

	Investment A		Investment B	
Year	Rate of Return	Year End Value	Rate of Return	Year End Value
1	10%	$110	20%	$120
2	10%	$121	−8%	$110
3	10%	$133	21%	$133

Chart 4

Starting to save early allows the power of compounding to work for you. Let's assume, for example, that your investment can earn 10% per year. If you start at age 25 and invest $1,000 each year (a total of $40,000), your investments will grow to $443,000 by the time you are 65. If you wait until you are 40 to start your program you will need to invest $4,500 each year (a total of $112,500) to have that much. Waiting the extra 15 years forces you to invest three times as much money to get the same result.

Is time important for risk?

Yes, it is. Risk can also be thought of as the volatility (ups and downs) in the investment's rate of return. Volatility occurs because returns often differ from period to period. The size of these changes determines your ability to predict the investment's future returns. The greater the changes, the harder it is to make accurate predictions.

Time, however, often acts to calm the volatility of investments and, therefore, makes them less risky. Many investments have very stable average annual returns over long periods of time even though their return in any one given year is quite unpredictable.

Stocks of large companies like IBM, General Motors, and Xerox are such investments. When professionals study stocks, they often use a collection (index) of these stocks known as the Standard and Poor's (S&P) 500. (We define stocks and indexes in Chapter 4, Equities.) Chart 5 shows that over long periods of time, the S&P 500 has a compound rate of return of around 13%.

Over shorter periods, the S&P 500 is hard to predict. 95% of the time (95 times out of 100), the average return for one year falls somewhere between minus 9.5% and plus 36%. The other 5% of the time, the return won't even be in this range. Over periods of ten years, the range is narrowed considerably. 95% of the time the average annual return falls between 6% and 20.4%.

S&P 500 Performance
(95% Ranges of Average Annual Compound Return)

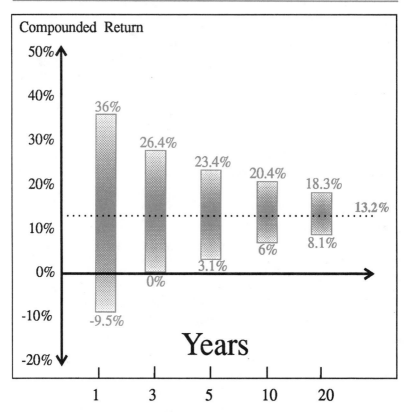

This chart was provided by Professors F.J. Gould and C.B. Garcia
of the University of Chicago's Graduate School of Business. The
analysis was based on S&P 500 returns from 1976 – 1991.

Chart 5

This means that if you invest $1,000 in the S&P 500 today,
you really have no idea what it will be worth next year.
You can, however, be pretty sure that, if the stock market's
long-term behavior does not change, in about 30 years it
will be worth about $40,000.

In other words, investments which seem risky in the short-term may not be all that risky in the long-term. This is very important for you, as a long-term investor, to understand.

How are risk and return related?

Riskier investments tend to give higher returns. This is why return and risk pull investment decisions in opposite directions. We want high returns, but we want low risk. Thus, we must learn to strike a balance between the two.

Is there any way to measure return and risk?

(Those of you not interested in the more mathematical aspects of investing may want to skip this question.)

As we said, returns are expressed as percentages. Risk can also be measured as a percentage. An investment's volatility (risk) is gauged by a statistic called the standard deviation. The standard deviation measures how much the returns deviate over time from their average. The larger the standard deviation, the more volatile are the returns and the riskier is the investment.

Investments A and B in Chart 4 provide interesting examples. Both investments have a compound rate of return of 10%. Investment A also has an average annual return of 10% with a standard deviation of 0 (meaning the return is constant from year to year). Investment B, however, has an average annual return of 11% with a standard deviation of 16.5%.[1] The higher standard deviation means that investment B is much riskier than investment A because its return varies considerably from year to year. While you can be sure that investment A will return 10% in any given year, investment B could earn much more or much less than 10%. In fact, it might even lose money.

(For a discussion of how the mean and standard deviation are calculated, refer to a statistics textbook. Many hand-held calculators are capable of doing these calculations.)

A standard measurement called the Sharpe ratio provides a risk-adjusted rate of return. It is an estimate of how much return an investment will yield per unit of risk. It is calculated by dividing the investment's mean (average) return by the standard deviation of its returns. The purpose of the Sharpe ratio is to put different investments on the same playing field. This ratio is useful when you are trying to determine which funds to include in your account because it gives you an idea of whether the returns reflect the investment manager's skill, the use of riskier assets, or just luck. The mean shows how well a fund performed over a certain time period, and the Sharpe ratio shows why. As a general rule, the greater the fund's Sharpe ratio, the more skilled is the manager.

---

[1] For an investment's compound return and average annual return to be equal, the investment must have the same return every year. If the returns of an investment fluctuate from year to year, the compound return will be slightly less than the average annual return. This is why investment B's average annual return is 11%, but its compound return is less, only 10%.

Chart 6 shows how the Sharpe ratio is used. Funds A, B, C, and D were followed for several years, and their mean returns, standard deviations, and Sharpe ratios are shown.

Four Imaginary Funds

	Fund			
	A	B	C	D
Mean	10%	15%	15%	15%
Standard Deviation	5%	10%	7.5%	5%
Sharpe Ratio	2	1.5	2	3

Chart 6

As you can see, fund B had a higher mean return than fund A, but its higher standard deviation resulted in a lower Sharpe ratio. This means that fund B's better performance seems to have been due to luck.

Fund C also had a higher return than fund A, but fund C's Sharpe ratio is the same as fund A's. This suggests that fund C's higher return was due to investing in riskier assets.

Fund D had both a higher return and a higher Sharpe ratio than fund A. This means that the higher return resulted from fund D's manager doing a better job at picking securities.

Chapter 3: Fixed-income Investments

What is a bond?

A bond is the IOU that is issued when a corporation or a government (federal, state, or local) borrows money from investors.

When I buy a government bond, am I actually lending money to the government?

That's correct. When you lend money, you are said to be investing in or buying a bond. The borrower is said to be issuing or selling the bond.

Does that mean the national debt exists because the federal government borrows money by selling bonds?

That's right. The federal government is indebted to the investors who buy government bonds. These investors-- individual citizens, companies, retirement plans--are from both the United States and abroad.

Why are bonds also called fixed-income investments?

Bonds are called fixed-income investments because every-thing is predetermined or fixed in advance. The investor knows when he will receive his interest payments, how much they will be, and when his principal (amount of the loan) will be repaid.[2]

How does a loan repayment schedule work?

Let's assume a $10,000 bond is for three years (has a three year maturity) and pays interest semi-annually (every six months) at an annual rate of 5%. For the next three years, the investor will receive a semi-annual interest payment of $250.[3] When the bond matures, she will get back her initial investment (principal of $10,000).

Do all fixed-income investments use this type of repayment schedule?

Mortgages, another type of fixed-income investment, often pay interest and a portion of the principal periodically. With some repayment schedules, the entire principal is repaid in installments. If the bond in the above example had this type of repayment schedule, the investor would receive $900 quarterly for three years. Other repayment schedules provide for only a portion of the principal to be repaid in installments. The balance is due at maturity.

---

[2] Some fixed income investments are issued with adjustable interest rates. This means that the interest rate changes periodically (monthly, quarterly, annually).

[3] A 5% annual interest rate is equal to a 2.50% semi-annual rate (5% divided by 2 equals 2.50%). The semi-annual interest payment is 2.50% of $10,000 or $250.

Other fixed-income investments (zero coupon bonds) do not make periodic payments. The interest accrues (accumulates) and is paid with the principal at maturity. If the $10,000 was invested in a zero coupon bond, the lump sum payment at maturity would be $11,576.

Why are these called zero coupon bonds?

In some cases, when an investor buys a bond, he actually receives a certificate with coupons attached to it. Each of these coupons represents an interest payment. When an interest payment is due, the investor clips off a coupon and sends it to the bond's issuer for payment. Since zero coupon bonds pay no interest until maturity, they don't have coupons, and this is why they are called zero coupon bonds.

What are convertible bonds?

These are corporate bonds which can be exchanged for stock in the issuing company.

Are there other types of fixed-income investments?

Yes, and they include guaranteed interest contracts (GICs) from insurance companies, bank investment contracts (BICs), bank certificates of deposit (CDs), mortgage backed securities, and money market instruments.

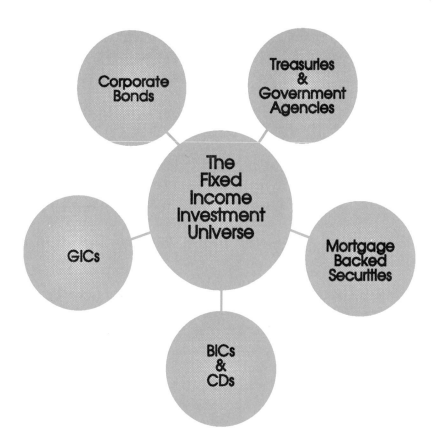

Since I get my principal back at maturity, aren't fixed-income investments risk free?

All investments have some risk. For example, a corporate borrower may go bankrupt or not have the money to make interest payments or repay the principal. This risk is called the credit or default risk, and its significance depends on who the borrower is. Other types of risk will be discussed later.

While not everyone agrees on exactly which types of fixed-income investments are riskier than others, the following summary should give you some idea.

United States Government Securities

Fixed-income investments issued by the federal government are risk free if held to maturity because they are backed by the "full faith and credit" of the United States. If sold before maturity, however, they are subject to the risk of rising interest rates. This risk is discussed later in this chapter.

Government bonds are classified by their maturities. Those with maturities of three, six, or twelve months are called Treasury bills or just T-bills. (T-bills and other very short-term investments are often called money market instruments, cash equivalents, or simply cash.) Treasury notes have maturities of one to ten years. Treasury bonds mature in ten to thirty years. The government also issues zero coupon bonds. T-bills and savings bonds are common examples.

The United States government also guarantees securities of federal agencies. Some examples are mortgage backed securities issued by the Government National Mortgage Association (Ginnie Mae) and the Federal National Mortgage Association (Fannie Mae).

Many government securities funds invest in Ginnie Mae's and Fannie Mae's as well as other securities backed by the U.S. government.

Certificates of Deposits (CDs) and Bank Investment Contracts (BICs)

CDs and BICs (CDs specifically designed for large retirement plans) are not risky if they are fully insured by the Federal Deposit Insurance Corporation (FDIC). The FDIC, an institution of the Federal Government, insures each of these deposits up to $100,000 per participant.[4] If the size of your account exceeds $100,000, however, the risk depends on the financial stability of the bank.

Insurance Company Guaranteed Investment Contracts (GICs)

The fixed-income investments sold by insurance companies are called GICs. The riskiness of a GIC depends on the financial stability of the insurance company. These companies, however, are regulated by state governments. Their financial stability and claims-paying ability are evaluated by independent rating organizations, so GICs from most insurers are usually considered safe investments.

Chart 7 compares the ratings systems of five of these independent rating organizations.

---

[4] The amount of FDIC protection extended to BICs is currently being reviewed by Congress and may change in the future.

Comparison of Ratings

	Standard and Poor's	Moody's	A.M. Best	Duff and Phelps	Weiss
Superior	AAA	Aaa	A++ A+	AAA	
Excellent	AA+ AA AA−	Aa1 Aa2 Aa3	A A−	AA+ AA AA−	A+ A A−
Good	A+ A A−	A1 A2 A3	B++ B+	A+ A A−	B+ B B−
Adequate	BBB+ BBB BBB−	Baa1 Baa2 Baa3	B B−	BBB+ BBB BBB−	C+ C C−
Below Average	BB+ BB BB−	Ba1 Ba2 Ba3	C++ C+	BB+ BB BB−	D+ D D−
Financially Weak	B+ B B−	B1 B2 B3	C C−	B+ B B−	E+ E E−
Nonviable	CCC CC D	Caa Ca C	D E F	CCC CC D	F

Chart 7

Do not misinterpret the term guaranteed however. Neither the federal government nor your employer backs this investment.[5] The guarantee comes solely from the insur-

---

[5] States have established guarantee (rescue) funds to protect life insurance and individual annuity policyholders. Many states also extend their protection to retirement plan participants, but the amount of coverage is usually limited. You can get the details from your state's insurance commission.

ance company. To avoid any misunderstanding as to the nature of the guarantee, GICs are often called steady asset funds, stable value assets, or stable fixed-income funds.

GICs have been quite popular because they have had higher returns than Treasuries and have been perceived as low risk. Also, in contrast to bonds, GICs do not fluctuate in value. (Why bonds fluctuate in value will be discussed shortly.) Their value, called book value, is equal to the money invested plus accrued interest.[6] When an employee retires, he gets book value. A problem with many GICs is that the amount of money that you can transfer out of them is limited.

Since a few large insurance companies have experienced financial problems and been taken over by their state's insurance commission, new products called synthetic GICs have been developed to reduce the default risk associated with traditional GICs. From the investor's standpoint, synthetic and traditional GICs appear identical. The difference between the two is the ownership of the assets which back the GIC. In a traditional GIC, the insurance company owns the assets. In a synthetic GIC, the assets belong to the plan participants.

---

[6] In the future, GICs might no longer be valued at book. They may have to be valued like other fixed income investments.

Corporate Bonds

Like GICs, the riskiness of these fixed-income investments depends on the financial condition of the company which issues them. If you buy a bond from a financially sound company, your risk will be quite low. If you invest in a bond issued by a financially weak or speculative company, your risk is much higher. Don't forget, however, that a company's financial health can change over time so that today's low risk bond can become tomorrow's high risk one.

Are corporate bonds also rated?

Organizations such as Standard and Poor's, Moody's, and Duff and Phelps evaluate corporate bonds using systems similar to those used to rate insurance companies. Bonds with the top four ratings (BBB or higher according to Standard and Poor's, Baa or higher according to Moody's) are considered investment grade. Those with lower ratings are called speculative grade or junk bonds. Junk bonds pay higher interest rates than investment grade bonds to compensate for their added risk.

Besides the risk that the borrower won't pay you back, is there any other kind of risk in fixed-income investments?

Yes, a fixed-income investment has a definite maturity--the initial investment is returned after a fixed period of time. If you buy a 30-year Treasury bond with an interest rate of 8%, for example, you are assured of getting 8% interest for 30 years. You are, however, planning to tie up your money for 30 years. If interest rates go up to 10%, you will miss the opportunity of investing at a higher rate.

If I have a bond earning 8% and interest rates go to 10%, can I sell the bond and reinvest the money at the higher rate?

People buy and sell fixed-income investments all the time. If you sell your bond, however, you might not get all of your original investment back. If interest rates have gone up to 10%, nobody wants a bond that pays only 8%. A prospective buyer wants one that pays 10%. To sell your 8% bond in a 10% market, you're going to have to discount it. That means selling it for less than the face value (par). If interest rates had gone down, however, you could sell your bond for more than par. This is called selling at a premium.

Chart 8 shows the effect of interest rates on the prices of Treasury notes and bonds. As you can see, as a bond gets closer to maturity, interest rates have less of an effect on its price.

$1,000 Bond With an 8% Coupon Rate

Years To Maturity	Price if Interest Rates Drop to 6%	Price if Interest Rates Rise to 10%
3	$1,054	$949
5	$1,085	$923
10	$1,149	$875
20	$1,231	$828

Chart 8

Could you give an example of selling at a discount?

Assume that you bought a thirty year Treasury bond with a 5% coupon fifteen years ago for $1,000. Since then, the bond has paid you $25 every six months. If you hold the bond until maturity, you will continue to receive interest payments. If you sell the bond, however, the remaining interest and the principal will be paid to the buyer.

If you want to sell the bond when new bonds are paying 7% interest, nobody is going to give you $1,000 for an old bond paying only 5%. To sell your bond, you will have to discount it and lose some of your principal.

How does a discount enable the new buyer to make up for the lower interest rate?

Discounting the bond to $816 will drive up its yield to maturity to 7%. The buyer will receive semi-annual payments of $25 giving the bond a current yield of 6.13% (2 times $25 divided by $816). At maturity, however, the buyer will receive the entire $1,000 face amount, not just the $816 he paid. This will push the yield to maturity up to 7.0%.

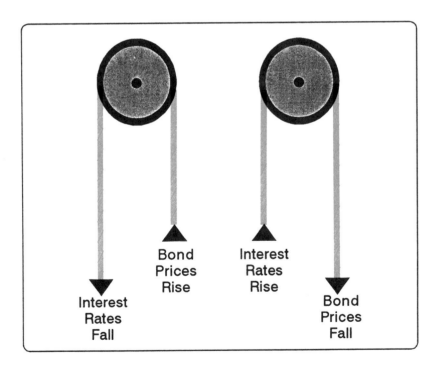

What are the differences between yield, yield to maturity, and total return?

Yield (or current yield) is the rate of interest you get based on what was paid for the bond. It is calculated by dividing the annual interest payment by the price you paid for the bond.

Yield to maturity recognizes that, even though you may not have paid par for the bond, you will still get the par value at maturity. Therefore, at maturity you will realize either a gain (if you bought the bond at a discount) or a loss (if you bought the bond at a premium).

Yield to maturity, rather than current yield, is used to price bonds. Yield to maturity and the bond price resulting from it are difficult to determine by hand but can be easily calculated using one of the many financial calculators available.

Total return includes changes in the bond's price and interest payments received during the specified period. Note, however, that the only way to realize any gain or loss from a change in the price of the bond is to sell the bond. The total return assumes that the bond is sold at the end of the period.

Do most people hold their bonds to maturity or do they sell them?

Many individual investors hold bonds to maturity. Fund managers, on the other hand, usually do not. They try to predict whether interest rates are going up or down and trade bonds accordingly.

The nuts and bolts of fixed-income investing, then, is guessing which direction interest rates will go in the future. If you think they will go up, you will want to buy fixed-income investments with relatively short maturities, so you can get your money back quickly and re-invest it at higher rates. If you think interest rates will go down, you will want longer maturities to lock in the high rate for as long as possible.

So long-term fixed-income investments expose me to greater risk than short-term bonds when interest rates are going up?

Yes, they do. And, since return follows risk, you should expect to get a higher yield to maturity on long-term investments than you get on short-term ones (at least when rates are expected to go up).

Are there any more risks in fixed-income investments?

Yes, there is the prepayment risk, and many investors don't understand it. When you buy a fixed-income investment, you assume that you can keep it until maturity.

But most corporate bonds are callable. That means the company can pay off the bond in full at any time after a certain date known as the call date. (It's like a mortgage: most of us are entitled to repay it in full at any time.) When that happens, the company is said to call the bond.

Bonds are usually called when interest rates go down and the company is able to reissue debt at a lower interest rate.

This is good for them but bad for you because the lower interest rates mean that you won't be able to earn as much anymore. Therefore, it is important for you to know if the bond you are investing in is callable.

Some other types of fixed-income investments, such as Ginnie Mae-backed mortgages, have a similar risk because the mortgage can be prepaid in full at any time.

How do fixed-income investments affect buying power?

Historically, the return on fixed-income investments has not been much greater than inflation. Chart 9 shows actual and inflation-adjusted returns for several fixed-income investments from 1960 to 1991. The inflation-adjusted return, or real return as it is often called, recognizes that some of the growth of the investment was due to inflation.

Inflation Adjusted Performance of Fixed–Income Investments

Asset Type	Maturity	Actual Annual Compound Rate of Return (1960 – 1991)	Inflation Adjusted Annual Compound Rate of Return (1960 – 1991)
T–Bills	1 month	6.36%	1.34%
Treasury Notes	5 years	7.72%	2.64%
Treasury Bonds	30 years	6.80%	1.76%
Corporate Bonds	30 years	7.26%	2.20%

Source: Ibbotson Associates, Chicago.

Chart 9

For example, five year Treasury notes had an annual compound rate of return of 7.72% from 1960 to 1991. The inflation-adjusted return, however, is only 2.64%. This means that 66% of the growth in Treasury notes during this period was due to inflation. It is the inflation-adjusted return which shows how little your buying power has increased.

Chapter 4: Equities

How do I invest in a company?

You invest in a company by buying that company's stock (equity).[7] The company then prepares a stock certificate showing how many shares you purchased. Those shares, taken as a percentage of the total number of outstanding shares,[8] are the portion of the company you own.

Do companies issue both bonds and stocks?

Yes. Companies issue stock when they want to raise money without taking on more debt. If, on the other hand, a company's board doesn't feel that investors will pay the price they want for new shares of stock, they sell bonds.

---

[7] There are two types of stock: common and preferred. This chapter focuses on common stock. Preferred stockholders are paid a fixed dividend (similar to an interest payment) and may or may not have voting rights. No dividends are paid to common stockholders until preferred stockholders have been paid. Convertible preferred stock is preferred stock which can be converted into (exchanged for) common stock.

[8] Outstanding shares are those which are owned by shareholders. Treasury shares are issued shares which the company is either waiting to sell or has repurchased from shareholders.

Companies also sell bonds when existing shareholders do not want their ownership interests diluted (reduced) through additional outstanding shares.

Can you compare stockholders to bondholders?

Bondholders are a company's creditors. The company owes them money and has promised to repay the loan with interest. Stockholders are the company's owners; they have invested in the company. They share in the company's profits and, to the extent of their investments, bear the burden of its losses. If a company has financial difficulties, bondholders are paid interest before stockholders receive dividends. Chart 10 summarizes the major differences between bondholders and stockholders.

Comparing Bondholders to Stockholders

	Bondholders	Stockholders
Relationship to Company	Creditors	Owners
Reason for Cash Distribution	Interest	Dividend
Share in Company's Profits and Losses	No	Yes
Right to Vote On Board Members and Key Issues	No	Yes

Chart 10

How do I share in the profits?

When a company makes money, it may plow the profits back into the business--spend more on research and development, buy more equipment, and increase inventory--enabling the company to grow. In other cases, however, it may distribute some or all of the profits to the shareholders.

Companies usually distribute profits in one of two ways. The first is to pay cash dividends. The company sends your retirement plan's trustee a check.[9] Its amount is based on the number of shares you own and the dividend rate per share.

The other way of distributing profits is to give stockholders more stock. This is known as declaring a stock dividend.

Can I determine a stock's value based on the dividends it pays?

There is no definitive relationship between a company's financial health and growth potential and the dividends it pays. Each company's board of directors determines its dividend policy, and different boards have different philosophies.

---

[9] A trustee is the individual, bank, or trust company that is responsible for holding the assets of a retirement plan. The trustee ensures that the assets benefit only plan participants and their beneficiaries.

Many of the fastest growing companies pay little or no dividends because profits are plowed back into the business. Even among larger, more mature companies, high dividends are not always a sign of big profits. These companies can dip into past profits to inflate their dividends in an attempt to keep stockholder confidence high.

The P/E ratio is often mentioned. What is it?

Professionals often use the "price to earnings" (P/E) ratio to help them determine if a stock is a good buy. The P/E ratio is usually calculated by dividing the price of the stock by its earnings per share over the last twelve months. For example, if a stock is selling for $50 per share and it had earnings of $5 per share over the past year, its P/E ratio is 10. (Sometimes, however, the calculation of the P/E ratio involves estimates of the stock's future earnings.)

Sometimes professionals feel that a stock's P/E ratio or the P/E ratio of the market as a whole is too high relative to its history. That means they think the stock or the market is overvalued. When this occurs, investors often sell their stocks to lock in their profits and reinvest the money elsewhere.

Keep in mind that P/E ratios are just one way of looking at things, and not necessarily the best way. (See pages 44-47 for other approaches.)

You said that, as an owner, I also get to share in any increase in the value of the company. How does that happen?

As a company prospers, more investors want to own shares. This drives up the stock's price.

Why would a stock's price go down?

Drops in stock prices can't always be explained. Remember, it's the law of supply and demand which actually determines a stock's price. If fewer investors want to buy a stock and more want to sell it, the price will drop.

Why do investors suddenly not like a stock?

Sometimes, it is because the company has, or investors fear it may, become less profitable. For example, cuts in defense spending usually result in price decreases in the stocks of defense contractors.

Other times, however, there is no apparent reason why stocks fall out of favor. Investors tend to jump on bandwagons, so once some investors decide to sell a stock, chances are others will follow suit for fear they will be left behind. They are afraid that the stock's price will drop and they will lose their gains.

An example of this is the decline in price of IBM stock after the second quarter of 1992. The company reported earnings that were 5 times higher than its second quarter earnings in 1991. Apparently, however, some investors had expected still higher earnings and, so, dumped the stock causing prices to fall.

How do I know what my stock is worth?

If you own a stock that is traded every day, you can get a good idea of its worth by looking in a newspaper.

When you look up a stock, you will see more than one price; exactly how many depends on the market and the newspaper. All of these prices refer to trading that occurred the previous day. The opening price was the first price at which a stock sold. The closing price is the last. The high is the highest price the stock traded that day, and the low is the lowest. You will also see a number (usually a fraction) with a plus or minus sign in front of it. This number represents the net change in the price of the stock from the previous day's closing price. For example, if you see a +3/4 next to a stock, that means the price of the stock rose 3/4 of a dollar, or 75 cents.

The only way to know exactly what your stock is worth, however, is to have a broker sell it and see what price it commands.

How does my broker sell the stock?

Stocks are bought and sold on the stock markets. Some of the more famous markets include the New York, American, London, and Tokyo Stock Exchanges and the OTC (over-the-counter) market.

The exchanges are centralized locations where traders gather to buy and sell stocks. The firm that your broker works for has traders on the floors of the exchanges. Your broker places orders to the traders telling them to buy or sell certain stocks and the traders execute the orders.

The OTC market is not centralized like the exchanges. Rather it is a nationwide network of dealers connected by telephones and computers who trade stocks and bonds directly with each other. Historically, stocks of smaller companies have traded on the OTC market while those of larger companies have traded on the exchanges.

What are the Dow Jones Industrial Average and the S&P 500?

There are several generally accepted indexes which are intended to reflect the overall state of the U.S. stock market. Perhaps two of the most well-known are the Dow Jones Industrial Average (DJIA) and the Standard & Poor's 500 (S&P 500).[10]

---

[10] Several fixed-income indexes also exist. These include the Salomon Brothers BIG Index which measures the overall performance of investment grade corporate bonds.

There are also indexes for foreign markets. Perhaps the two most well known are the Nikkei which reflects the overall health of the Tokyo stock market and the EAFE which measures the overall performance of the European, Australian, and Far Eastern stock markets.

The DJIA consists of stocks of 30 industrial companies. The S&P 500 is a collection of stocks of 500 leading large companies from different sectors of the economy. It is a favorite index among many investors because the stocks it contains represent about 70% of the U.S. stock market's total value.

On the other hand, many investors feel that the S&P 500 is not a good gauge of the entire market because, even though it represents a large part of the total capital in the market, it does not include the stocks of small and mid-sized companies. These people think that indexes like the Wilshire 5000 are better indicators of the overall state of the market. The Wilshire 5000 includes all of the stocks on the New York and American Stock Exchanges and about 2000 OTC issues.

The techniques employed to calculate these indexes are beyond the scope of this guide. It is worth mentioning, however, that all of these indexes are calculated in such a way as to ensure comparability over time.

Are stocks riskier than bonds?

Yes, stocks are usually riskier. This is primarily because the stock markets have historically been more volatile than the bond markets. Furthermore, since bonds have fixed maturities and interest payment schedules, you know when you are going to get your money. With stocks, on the other hand, you do not know how much you will receive in dividends or if you will even get your original investment back.

Since stocks are riskier than bonds, and risk and return go hand in hand, does that mean that I will do better by investing mainly in stocks?

Yes, you will probably earn more with stocks. No one can guarantee that any particular stock will increase in value, but history shows convincingly that, on average, a diversified portfolio of stocks will produce a much greater return than a portfolio of fixed-income investments over time.

Stocks, Bonds, and Inflation (1960–1991)

Asset Type	Annual Compound Rate of Return	Growth of One Dollar
S&P 500 (Large Stocks)	10.42%	$23.85
Small Stocks	13.77%	$61.99
T–Bills	6.36%	$7.20
Treasury Notes	7.72%	$10.80
Treasury Bonds	6.80%	$8.21
Corporate Bonds	7.26%	$9.42
Inflation	4.95%	$4.69

Source: Ibbotson Associates, Chicago.

Chart 11

Chart 11 compares the returns of short, intermediate, and long-term fixed-income investments with those of the S&P 500 and small stocks. It also shows what would have happened if you had invested $1 in each of these asset classes at the beginning of 1960. The comparison is striking.

As we discussed previously, fixed-income investments historically have only slightly outpaced inflation. (See Chart 9 in Chapter 3.) Stocks, on the other hand, have outperformed inflation by a greater margin. This is an important comparison, because only investments which do better than inflation increase your buying power and contribute substantially to your retirement nest egg.

If I decide to invest in stocks, which stocks should I buy?

That's the million dollar question. No one knows for sure if a stock's price will go up or down or by how much. In fact, market forecasters often miss the boat when making predictions for the stock and bond markets as a whole, let alone for individual securities.

You, however, can develop a strategy that reflects your goals. Your employer has carefully selected an array of funds from which you can choose. We will discuss these shortly, but first we should introduce you to some of the different styles (strategies) professionals use when investing in stocks.

Style 1: Market Capitalization

Some professionals like to invest in either large cap, mid-cap, or small cap companies. Cap is short for capitalization: the total dollar amount of all the securities issued by a company. While there are no exact definitions, companies are often considered large cap if they have a market capitalization of more than about $3 billion. Small cap companies are often defined as those with a market capitalization of less than about $500 million. Midcap companies fall in between. There are periods when one size of companies vastly outperforms the others, as shown in Chart 12.

Small vs. Large Cap Total Returns

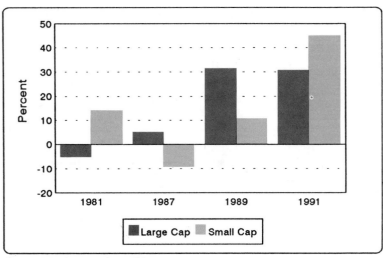

Source: Ibbotson Associates, Chicago.

Chart 12

Style 2: Capital Appreciation

Capital appreciation stocks are expected by stock market gurus to have above average growth in their market price.

Capital appreciation can be achieved by investing in either growth or value stocks. Growth stocks are the stocks of companies whose sales and earnings are increasing more quickly than the general economy and most other stocks.

Value stocks are those whose intrinsic value (true worth) is greater than their market value. For example, the value of a company's assets (real estate, equipment, patents, etc.) may be greater than the total price of all of its outstanding stock.

For some reason, however, the market has overlooked these value stocks. Contrarians, the people who find and buy these stocks, purchase them at what they consider bargain prices. When the rest of the market realizes the value stock's worth, demand will increase, driving up prices. Then, contrarians hope, they can sell the stock at considerable profit.

Style 3: Income

Income stocks are expected to pay above average dividends. They are often less volatile than capital appreciation stocks but usually lack much growth potential.

Stocks which are categorized as one type today may be classified as a different type in the future. For example, today's growth stock may be tomorrow's value or income stock.

Style 4: Rotational Analysis

Some investment professionals, called sector rotators, divide American industry into various groups or sectors. They further break each sector into groups and subgroups. Sector rotators then invest in the subsectors they expect to do well.

For example, if a sector rotator feels that the financial sector has good near-term prospects, she will buy stock in banks and insurance companies. If she feels the media sector will do poorly, she will sell her holdings in broadcasting and publishing companies.

Style 5: Defensive

Another more cautious approach to investing is the defensive style. Defensive investors buy stocks of two types of companies: very large corporations which have the resources to weather hard times, and firms in industries which are usually not affected much by market downswings. While these stocks are a good defense against losing money in a recession, they usually don't gain much during good times.

Style 6: Market Timing

Some investment managers think that they can predict the direction the stock and bond markets are going to take. When they think the stock market will go up, they shift their money from fixed-income investments into the stocks. When they think that stocks are going to go down, they sell their stocks to lock in profits and move their money back into fixed-income investments. Sometimes these managers feel that the best place to be is in cash (money market securities).

Many studies have shown, however, that the movement of the stock and bond markets can't be predicted consistently. This leads to the conclusion that the stock market is not a place to make a quick buck. It is, rather, a place to invest for the long-term.

A study by the editors of Fortune magazine (Fortune's 1986 Investors' Guide, Fall 1985, page 14) shows why market timing is so hard. If your timing is off, you are out of luck. If you had invested $100 in the S&P 500 in January of 1975, it would have grown to $395 by December of 1984 (a period of 40 quarters). If you had shifted your money out of the market for just three of those quarters (the first and second quarters of 1975 and the last quarter of 1982), your investment would have been worth only $248. This is just $10 more than what your money would have grown to had it been invested only in T-bills for the entire period. As you recall, T-bills are virtually risk free.

What are bull markets and bear markets?

Bull markets are extended periods of high overall stock returns. Bear markets are just the opposite: long periods of poor stock market performance.

Is there an advantage to investing in foreign stock markets?

Since foreign stock markets account for 60% of the total worldwide market value (capitalization) of all publicly traded stocks, foreign stocks are an asset class which should not be ignored. There are two advantages to international investing--added diversification and the opportunity for higher returns. If the U.S. stock market has a bad year and you are invested only in it, you will suffer a loss or, at best, make only a small gain. If, however, you are also invested in foreign markets, their performance may offset your losses in the U.S. market.

The World's Stock Markets

Year	U.S. Stock Market	Major Non–U.S. Stock Markets	Year	U.S. Stock Market	Major Non–U.S. Stock Markets
1967	+23%	+12%	1980	+23%	+19%
1968	+10%	+28%	1981	−9%	−5%
1969	−13%	+3%	1982	+15%	−5%
1970	+1%	−14%	1983	+17%	+21%
1971	+10%	+26%	1984	+1%	+5%
1972	+13%	+33%	1985	+27%	+53%
1973	−19%	−17%	1986	+13%	+67%
1974	−31%	−26%	1987	+1%	+23%
1975	+30%	+31%	1988	+12%	+27%
1976	+19%	0%	1989	+27%	+9%
1977	−12%	+15%	1990	−6%	−25%
1978	0%	+29%	1991	+27%	+10%
1979	+8%	+2%	1992	+4%	−14%

Chart 13

This can be seen in Chart 13 which compares annual returns of the Morgan Stanley U.S. Index with the Morgan Stanley Capital International Europe, Australia, New Zealand, and Far East (EAFE) Index. The latter index measures all of the major foreign stock markets.

Is there any correlation between the performance of fixed-income and equity investments?

While some money managers believe that the two are linked through various factors such as interest rates, much academic research and studies of actual performance have failed to show a definite relationship that can be consistently exploited.

I've heard about options and futures. What are they?

Options and futures are sophisticated financial tools which go beyond the ordinary buying and selling of investments.

Options give investors the right to buy (call option) or sell (put option) a fixed amount of a security at a predetermined price during a specified time period.

Futures are contracts in which investors agree to buy or sell a fixed amount of a security or commodity on a specific date. Trading in futures is somewhat similar to ordering merchandise through a catalog in that you agree to pay for and receive the merchandise at some time in the future rather than when the order is made.

Your retirement plan probably doesn't permit you to use options or futures, but the professionals who manage your stock and bond funds might. Options and futures can be used conservatively (to lock in profits or protect against losses) or aggressively (to try to enhance returns). Many of the uses of options and futures are highly technical, risky, and complex and are beyond the scope of this guide.

Chapter 5: Fund Investment

We've talked about stocks and bonds, but how do I apply this to the funds that I can invest in?

When you invest in a fund, you get two benefits: professional managers pick the individual securities and you get to own a wider variety of securities than you could purchase on your own. This diversification protects you against big losses if a single company goes bankrupt. Since funds behave like the securities in which they invest, understanding the way individual securities behave enables you to understand the behavior of funds.

Funds have a variety of names. When a bank runs a fund, it's called a commingled account. Separate accounts are funds which are run by insurance companies. And when an investment company runs such a fund, it's called a mutual fund. But in every case, you must ask: What types of securities does the fund invest in and what investment style does it use?

Do any funds invest in both stocks and bonds?

Yes, balanced and asset allocation funds invest in both equity and fixed-income investments. Asset classes (equities, fixed-income, and cash) perform differently over different time periods. The managers of balanced and asset allocation funds think they can predict the relative performance of different asset classes over the foreseeable future and adjust their portfolios accordingly.

What's the difference between balanced and asset allocation funds?

Managers of balanced funds try to find a compromise between the higher returns and higher risks of equities and the lower returns and lower risks of fixed-income investments. Traditional balanced fund managers are usually required to maintain a minimum amount of both stocks and bonds. This protects the fund from big losses due to being overexposed to one asset class.

Asset allocation managers, on the other hand, invest heavily in the asset class they think will do the best over the foreseeable future. In contrast to balanced funds, asset allocation funds are usually not required to have minimum amounts invested in stocks and bonds. The ability to switch freely among asset classes theoretically allows asset allocation funds to outperform pure stock funds. In reality, this isn't always the case.

The goal of balanced funds, then, is to seek steady and stable growth. Asset allocation funds, on the other hand, try to maximize returns and worry much less about volatility. The difference between asset allocation and balanced funds, however, is often blurred. This is because many investors and mutual funds use the terms balanced and asset allocation interchangeably.

Can I create my own balanced or asset allocation fund?

You can create a balanced fund only if your plan allows you to pick individual securities. You can, however, allocate your money among several stock, bond, and money market funds. This creates a portfolio that is similar to a balanced or an asset allocation fund.

Is allocating your money among different types of funds a form of diversification?

Yes, we previously discussed how investing in a mutual fund provides a diversified portfolio. Allocating your money among stock, bond, and money market funds gives you even more diversification. This type of diversification protects your portfolio from losses when one asset class does poorly.

The Case For Diversification

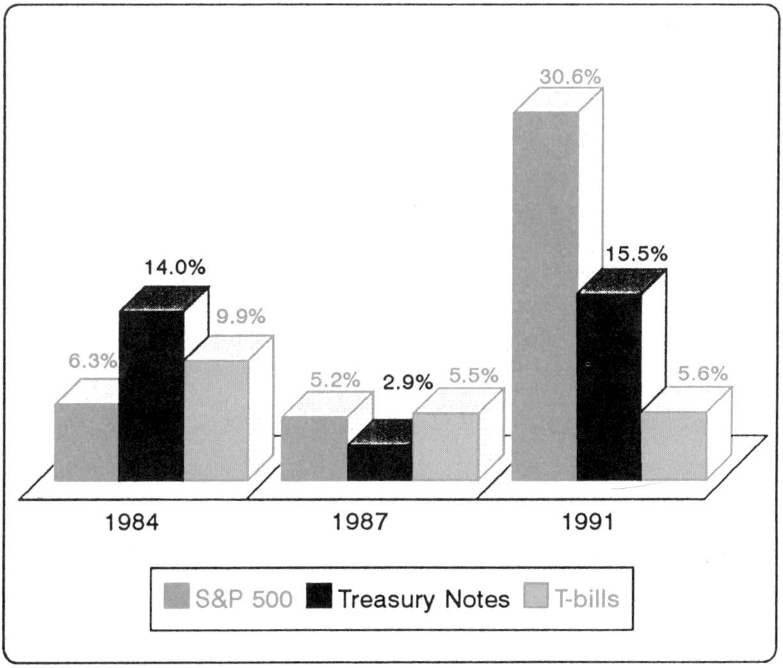

Source: Ibbotson Associates, Chicago.

Chart 14

Since different asset classes do better in different years (as can be seen in Chart 14), spreading your investments among asset classes results in more steady growth.

Chart 15 shows the levels of diversification in a typical retirement plan participant's portfolio. This structure protects the investor from big losses due to poor performance in a single asset class, fund, or security.

Levels of Diversification

		Your Portfolio	
Asset Class	Stocks	Fixed Income	Cash
Investment Options	Stock Funds / Employer Stock	Bond Funds / GIC & BIC Funds	Money Market Funds
Within Funds	Many Individual Securities		

Chart 15

What are index funds?

In an actively managed fund, the manager picks securities based on his expectations for the future. In contrast, index funds are passively managed. These funds are designed to mirror the performance, good or bad, of an index such as the S&P 500. To accomplish this, index funds invest in all or a scientifically selected sample of the stocks which make up the index.

For example, many S&P 500 index funds own virtually all of the stocks which comprise the S&P 500. Midcap and small stock index funds, on the other hand, invest in only a portion of the stocks in the index they track. Investors are attracted to index funds when they feel picking good managers consistently is difficult.

Bond index funds and index funds designed to simulate a specific investing style, such as small-cap value or high-cap growth, also exist.

How do I know what my funds are worth?

You will periodically receive a statement giving you the value of your shares. If you invest in a mutual fund that is available to the general public, you can also look up its price in the newspaper. (Not all mutual funds offered through retirement plans are available to the public.)

The exact price reporting format varies among newspapers. Usually the first column is labelled NAV or net asset value.

This is the price at which the mutual fund company will repurchase (redeem) your shares.[11]

Some funds, however, have deferred sales charges. If your fund has these, the amount you receive will be less than you would have expected based on the NAV. It is important to read the sales material (prospectus) to see if a fund has such a charge.[12]

The next column will be labelled offer price. This is what it costs to buy new shares of the fund. If the fund has no front end sales charge, this column will contain either NL (no load) or the same price as the NAV column. If the fund does impose a sales charge, the offer price exceeds the NAV by the amount of the sales charge.

---

[11] Open-end mutual funds shares, the kind most likely offered through your retirement plan, are not traded like stocks and bonds. They must be bought from and redeemed by the company that runs the fund. The company issues shares to meet demand. With closed-end mutual funds, on the other hand, the company issues a fixed number of shares which are then traded on the exchanges.

[12] Mutual funds which assess sales charges are called load funds. Those which do not are called no-load funds. Loads can be front-end and/or rear-end. Front-end loads are assessed when you buy shares. Rear-end loads are charged if shares are redeemed before a specified time period is over. Some funds have both types of loads.

There will probably also be a column which shows how much the NAV changed that day. For example, if this column has a +0.10 in it, then the NAV has increased 10 cents. If the column contains a -0.05, the NAV has dropped 5 cents.

Chapter 6: Asset Allocation

Never make predictions, especially about the future.
--Yogi Berra

Now that I understand the basics of investing, how do I apply my new knowledge?

The asset allocation process is where you put everything you have learned to use.

What is asset allocation?

Asset allocation is the process of dividing your savings among your investment options. You should periodically review and possibly reallocate your existing accounts. You may also want to change how future contributions will be invested. Many investment professionals feel that asset allocation is responsible for 90% of a portfolio's performance over time.

Will I be able to predict with a high degree of certainty which assets will do well in the foreseeable future?

We all wish we had a crystal ball that would answer that question. Unfortunately, we don't. Each year major business publications poll leading economists and investment professionals for their opinions as to where interest rates and the stock market are heading. Their responses vary dramatically and often contradict each other. This inability to accurately predict the short-term is why asset allocation is so important.

If the experts have trouble predicting the future, how can I wisely allocate my retirement savings?

Perhaps the most common mistake people make is believing that they need to predict which asset class will do better over the short-term. This guessing focuses attention on the likelihood of losing money and not on goals. By using common sense anyone should be able to make intelligent investment choices.

Any allocation strategy must:

1. assume the future will resemble the past;

2. incorporate your sources of retirement income;

3. consider how long you have until retirement;[13]

4. balance fear and greed;

5. strive for an income that outperforms inflation.

How will the future resemble the past?

Over the long-term, stocks have outperformed bonds. Professional money managers believe this trend will

---

[13]   This discussion assumes that you will not need money until retirement. If you will need some of the money earlier (perhaps to educate your children), you may want to invest more in bonds and money market instruments.

continue in the future. Remember, the greater the risk, the greater the return.

When we discuss stocks, bonds, and cash, we are, unless otherwise stated, referring to markets as a whole or a diversified portfolio of these investments.

Why is it important to know the sources of my retirement income?

Let's look at Bob and Mary. Both are 40 and their incomes are the same. They also contribute the same amount to their self-directed retirement plans. Bob's employer also provides him with a significant pension benefit. Mary's employer, however, cannot afford a pension plan. Bob's self-directed retirement plan is like icing on a cake. Mary's plan, however, is the cake itself. Bob's situation is such that he can place a much heavier emphasis on safety of principal than Mary can.

Please explain that further.

Charts 16a and 16b present a general philosophy on investing. According to this approach, at 40 both should be heavily invested in stocks. Since the self-directed retirement plan is Mary's only retirement nest egg, she must maximize growth. If her income goals are not met, she is out of luck.

Bob's pension will provide a significant portion of his retirement income. His self-directed retirement plan is a means of making up any shortfall between his income goal and the pension benefit. Bob, then, can probably meet his goals with much lower returns than Mary can.

A Framework For Making Investment Decisions

Age	Objective	Reason
30–50	Maximum Growth	You can afford the extra risk because there is plenty of time before retirement to recoup short–term losses.
50–60	1) Conservative Growth 2) Minimize Chance of Big Losses 3) Gradually Reduce Stock Holdings	Since retirement is approaching, you want to start stabilizing you account. However, there is still time to recoup some losses.
60–65	1) Preservation of Account Balance 2) Some Stocks Retained as an Inflation Hedge	Retirement is right around the corner. You should avoid taking risks because you might not have time to recoup losses. However, you still need to maintain your buying power.

Chart 16a

Age	Stocks	Bonds
30–50	60–100%	0–40%
50–60	40–60% (Gradually Reduce Over Time)	40–60%
60–65	20–30%	70–80%

Chart 16b

If Bob lives to a ripe old age, won't inflation have eroded much of his buying power?

That's a good point. Most people are like Bob and do not consider inflation. Chart 17 shows how much annual income a person who retired in 1970 needed to maintain his original $30,000 of buying power.

Keeping Up With Inflation

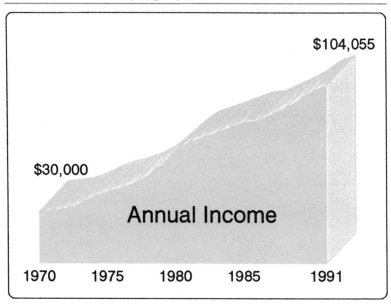

Chart 17

Bob, like Mary, should realize that time is on his side, losses will be made up, and he should go for growth. Worrying too much about losing money at age 40 will likely set the stage for financial difficulties later.

Since Mary has only one source of retirement income, shouldn't she be more concerned with safety of principal than Bob?

You're probably thinking that, since Mary does not have the cushion of a pension benefit, she is not in a position to gamble with her retirement account. Your idea may be that she must be conservative and make sure she does not lose money.

Remember, though, Mary has 25 years until retirement. We have seen that, over the long-term, equities are not all that risky and have historically provided much better returns than bonds. These better returns have occurred despite stocks being much more volatile than bonds.

Are you saying that diversified long-term stock market investors will incur losses but that these losses will usually be recouped?

This is exactly what I'm saying. Diversified long-term stock market investors have been well rewarded in spite of temporary setbacks. If time is on your side, diversified stock market investing should not be viewed as gambling.

Everything you say makes sense for someone who's forty. But what about those of us who are now in our early fifties?

While retirement is not necessarily just around the corner, it is not all that far off. At this age it is probably wise to begin gradually moving some assets out of stocks and into less volatile bonds. But remember, if you have 12 to 15 years until retirement, you may still want to have a substantial portion of your investments in stocks (see Charts 16a and 16b).

Why do we want to start moving into bonds as we near retirement?

If you invest in short and intermediate term government and high-grade corporate bond funds, your default risk is nonexistent (government) or minimal (corporate). Assuming interest rates don't skyrocket, you can't lose much money.

With stocks, on the other hand, you can lose a lot of money in short time periods. For example, during 1992, shares of IBM ranged in value from a high of 100 3/8 to a low of 45 7/8.

By being overly cautious, aren't we running the risk of missing out on a bull market?

Yes, the stock market may do quite well over that period and, in hindsight, we will wish we had invested in it. On the other hand, the market may do poorly, and we will be very happy we weren't in it. This uncertainty is why the stock market is not a good investment vehicle if you have a short time horizon.

You must balance the fear of major losses against the possibility of scoring big. Using common sense has always been important, but it is even more so now. For example, if interest rates are rising, you would not want to move into long-term bonds because you could possibly lose more money in them than in the stock market. (See Chart 8 in Chapter 3.) Money market and short and intermediate term bond funds would be the options to consider. Your choice or choices would depend upon what options your plan offers, their different yields, and how high you think interest rates (inflation) will go. On the other hand, if interest rates look as if they will drop considerably, a long-term bond fund might be your best choice.

Should we stay in stocks if interest rates are very low and the stock market looks fine?

You must define what "looking fine" means. But your point is a good one. You may be better off remaining in stocks. It is because of situations like these that Chart 16b shows ranges rather than specific percentages. Only you can make these decisions. Don't expect your employer to act as your investment advisor.

Have you forgotten people who work for companies that only recently installed a retirement plan? Many of them are in their early fifties with only small account balances.

Our discussion also applies to them. However, these individuals should seriously consider a balanced fund. The advantage of this approach is that a professional money manager will perform the allocation process after evaluating current economic conditions. Presumably her training and experience will produce better decisions than those of non-investment oriented individuals. This know-how is most important when there are relatively few years to go until retirement.

Are you saying that a person just starting to invest at age 50 should adopt a different strategy from a 50 year old who has been investing for some time?

Usually this is the case. A 50 year old who has been investing since he was 40 has probably learned to weather the ups and downs of the stock market. A 50 year old who has never invested in the stock market is likely to panic over short-term losses. He feels he won't have enough time to recoup the losses. This may cause him to invest emotionally rather than rationally, which will probably result in poor decisions.

Are you saying that emotions play an important role in the investment process?

Absolutely, some investors are paralyzed by even the thought of losing money. Others are risk seekers; they are comfortable with riskier investment positions.

This chapter is directed toward the optimistic-yet-realistic investor. (See Chapter 1: Types of Investors.) While no two investors have the same attitude toward risk, optimistic-yet-realistic investors take the middle ground. They incorporate historical performance into their decisions, develop strategies, and are willing to change course if appropriate.

Please summarize the asset allocation process.

The ultimate goal of asset allocation is to provide an inflation adjusted income so that you may live comfortably during retirement. Asset allocation, however, cannot work miracles. The earlier you start saving and the larger are your contributions, the greater is the likelihood that your retirement goals will be met.

Remember that over long periods of time stocks outperform bonds and cash. Furthermore, when you invest for the long haul, and do not jump in and out of the market, stocks are not all that risky--the ups generally more than compensate for the downs.

Patience and common sense are essential for successful investing. No one has a perfect crystal ball. This is why Charts 16a and 16b were developed. These charts are guides, not perfect solutions. They are like the recipe for a good dish. Just as the chef modifies the recipe to meet her tastes, so should you tailor the strategy presented in these charts to meet your needs. Finally, concentrate on obtaining your financial goals. Do not become preoccupied with how much money you can lose.

Remember, also, the importance of diversification. This is best summarized by the well-respected consultant to institutional investors, Peter Bernstein: "Diversification is the only rational deployment against our ignorance."

Chapter 7: Dollar-Cost Averaging

How do I know when to invest?

The best day of the year to invest is the day that prices are the lowest. The problem is picking that day. Over the long run, however, investing on the best day is often not that much better than investing on an average day or even the worst day. Chart 18 shows how much money you would have earned by investing $5,000 on the best and worst possible days of each year for the past twenty years.[14]

Time, Not Timing, is the Key to Success

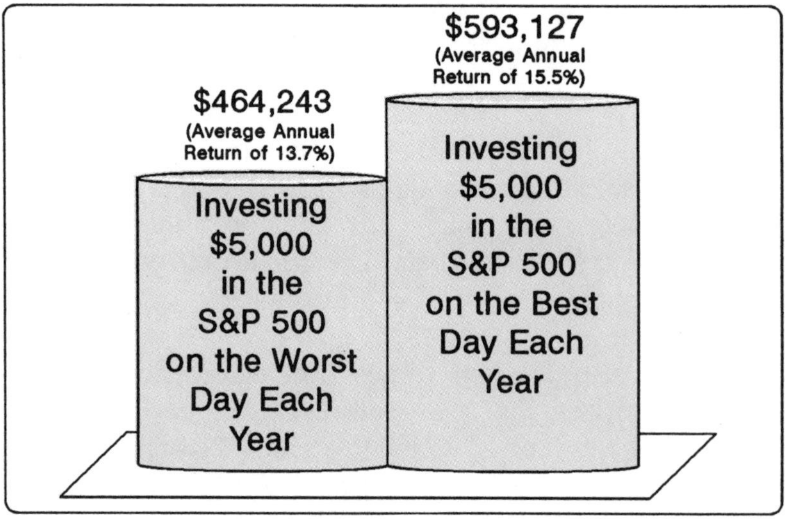

$593,127
(Average Annual
Return of 15.5%)

$464,243
(Average Annual
Return of 13.7%)

Investing
$5,000
in the
S&P 500
on the Worst
Day Each
Year

Investing
$5,000
in the
S&P 500
on the Best
Day Each
Year

Chart 18

---

[14] Data taken from <u>The American Funds Investor</u> (Autumn 1992).

Are you saying that any day is a good day to invest?

Yes, if you are investing specified monthly amounts into each fund. This technique is called dollar-cost averaging. It is a systematic approach which takes the guessing out of investing. You invest the same dollar amount every month regardless of whether prices go up or down. This way, you automatically buy more shares when prices are low and less when they're high.

An example of dollar-cost averaging is shown in Chart 19. A participant invested $300 monthly for one year. At year's end, he accumulated 424 shares at an average price per share of $8.49.[15] This price is 16.7% less than the average of the share prices at the beginning of each month ($10.20). At this price, he would have only purchased 353 shares.

---

[15] $8.49 = the total amount invested ($3,600) divided by the total number of shares purchased (424).

The Mechanics of Dollar–Cost Averaging

Month	Price per Share	Shares Bought
January	$10.00	30
February	$15.00	20
March	$5.00	60
April	$7.50	40
May	$5.00	60
June	$15.00	20
July	$12.50	24
August	$10.00	30
September	$15.00	20
October	$7.50	40
November	$5.00	60
December	$15.00	20
Investor's Average Share Price	$8.49	424
Average Monthly Share Price	$10.20	353

The fluctations in this example are dramatic. It is unlikely that any real investment would experience such volatility on a monthly basis. Such large fluctuations are used to demonstrate, in a simple example, how dollar–cost averaging benefits the long–term investor.

Chart 19

If I use dollar-cost averaging, how do I change my asset mix?

With dollar-cost averaging, you are investing a specified amount monthly into each fund. When you wish to reallocate your future contributions, you simply change your monthly investment in each fund.

You can also use dollar-cost averaging to change your current fund balances. Rather than making the changes all at one time, move money among the funds in equal amounts over a predetermined period.

What do I do with the money once I retire?

Some people will roll their money into an IRA and continue to invest in the same types of funds they invested in through their retirement plan. Others may want to try their hand at picking stocks and bonds. In either case, they take money out of the IRA as needed or required by federal law.

Other retirees, not wanting to make investment decisions, buy annuities from insurance companies. With a traditional annuity the insurance company pays a stream of fixed payments at specific intervals (eg. monthly or yearly). The annuity option you select will determine the amount of the payments and how long they will last. For example, they may go on for as long as you or your spouse is alive or they may stop after 10 years.

Variable annuities provide fluctuating (variable) payments. When you buy a variable annuity, you can invest in several separate accounts. In return, you get annuity units (similar to shares of a mutual fund), the value of which fluctuates with the returns of the separate account. Each month you get a payment based on the number of annuity units you hold and the value of each unit. Variable annuities are riskier than traditional annuities but also provide the potential for higher payments to help keep pace with inflation.

Chapter 9: Your Investment Options

After reading this guidebook, I felt confident that I could make sensible investment decisions. When I reviewed my options, however, I got confused. I encountered terms which you never discussed. What's going on?

You're facing a communications problem, not an investment problem. For example, many stock funds are called growth funds whether the manager follows the growth or value style to select stocks. Other funds, such as the famous Magellan, Wellington, and Washington Mutual funds, have names that don't reflect (unless you are a mind reader) either their manager's style or the types of securities in which they invest.

So how do I know what are a fund's philosophy and style?

You must read the material that is distributed by the investment managers. This includes the prospectuses, annual and quarterly reports, economic outlooks, and investment commentaries. This information should answer most of your questions. If you need additional information, call the investment management firm that runs the fund.

Please define some of the commonly used terms which I might encounter.

Chart 20 is a guide to most of the fund types you will encounter. Please keep in mind, however, that no manager designs a fund to exactly follow someone else's arbitrary definitions.

Classifying Investment Options

Fund Type	Investments	Objectives
Asset Allocation (Flexible Portfolio)	Stocks, Bonds, and Money Market	Maximum Annual Return
Balanced	Stocks, Bonds, and Money Market	Consistent Growth
Bond	Corporate and Government Bonds	Income With Preservation of Principal
Capital Appreciation	Stocks	Maximum Long–term Growth (Income and Volatility are not Considerations)
Global	U.S. and Non–U.S. Stocks and Bonds	Similar to Those of Funds Which Invest in U.S. Securities
Government Securities	Bonds and Mortgage Backed Securities Issued By the U.S. Government and its Agencies	Income With Preservation of Principal
Growth	Stocks	Long–term Growth (Not as Aggressive as Capital Appreciation Funds)
Income	Stocks Only, Bonds Only, or a Combination	High Current Income
International	Non–U.S. Stocks and Bonds	Similar to Those of Funds Which Invest in U.S. Securities
Steady Asset	GICs and BICs	Consistent Growth With No Market Value Fluctuations

Chart 20

My plan offers company stock as an option. How does that fit into my allocation strategy?

Purchasing your employer's stock is another equity option. It is important to realize, however, that investing in your employer's stock is not the same as investing in a diversified stock fund. Although this option is highly valued by employees, investing in a single stock, regardless of the company, is riskier than investing in a diversified stock fund.

Conclusion

Planning for your retirement is one of the most important things you will ever do. The investment decisions you make could dramatically affect the quality of your life after you retire.

No perfect formulas exist for investing. No rules are cast in stone. Experts often disagree, and professionals routinely give conflicting advice. Hopefully, however, this guide has given you an understanding of the basics and has started you on the road to making good investment decisions.

If you want to learn more about investing, you can find many good books on the subject at your local library. You may even want to take an evening course on investing at an area university. The more you know about investing, the greater is the likelihood of enjoying a secure retirement.

Appendix A: The Advantage of Starting Early

Only 38% of a retiree's income comes from social security.[16]

Chart 21 shows the monthly contributions required to accumulate $250,000 by age 65 if your savings grow at various rates. For example, if you start saving when you are 35 and earn a 7% rate of return, you will need to invest $205 per month.

Accumulating $250,000 By Age 65

| Starting | Growth Rate | | | |
Age	5%	7%	9%	11%
25	$164	$95	$53	$29
35	$300	$205	$137	$89
45	$608	$480	$374	$289
55	$1,610	$1,444	$1,292	$1,152

Chart 21

---

[16] Source: Susan Grad, Income of the Population 55 or Older, 1988, U.S. Department of Health and Human Services, Social Security Administration.

Chart 22 shows how much you will accumulate by making specified monthly investments if the growth rate is 7% or 9%. For example, if you start investing $300 a month when you are 45 and earn 9%, you will accumulate $200,366 by the time you are 65.

Your Retirement Nest Egg at Age 65

Monthly Savings	Start at Age 25		Start at Age 35	
	7% Annual Return	9% Annual Return	7% Annual Return	9% Annual Return
$200	$524,963	$936,264	$243,994	$366,148
$300	$787,444	$1,404,396	$365,991	$549,223
$400	$1,049,925	$1,872,528	$487,988	$732,297
$500	$1,312,407	$2,340,660	$609,985	$915,372
$600	$1,574,888	$2,808,792	$731,983	$1,098,446

Monthly Savings	Start at Age 45		Start at Age 55	
	7% Annual Return	9% Annual Return	7% Annual Return	9% Annual Return
$200	$104,185	$133,577	$34,617	$38,703
$300	$156,278	$200,366	$51,925	$58,054
$400	$208,371	$267,155	$69,234	$77,406
$500	$260,463	$333,943	$86,542	$96,757
$600	$312,556	$400,732	$103,850	$116,109

Chart 22

Appendix B: An Example of Asset Allocation

This example shows how one employee developed his investment strategies and why he decided to be an optimistic-yet-realistic investor.

Joe is 35, married, and has three children. Since retirement is far off (30 years), Joe views himself as a long-term investor. He realizes, however, some money might be needed sooner for an emergency or to educate a child. Joe also would like his portfolio (all of his investments) to outperform inflation. He concludes, however, that although real (inflation adjusted) long-term growth should be his main goal, some money should be free from market value fluctuations (price changes) in case it is unexpectedly needed.

This is only an example. The strategy Joe chose may not be appropriate for you. No single investment strategy fits all investors. What you decide should reflect your goals, risk tolerance, and financial situation (e.g. possible needs for loans, whether or not your spouse also has a retirement program, possible inheritances, etc.).

Many investment professionals feel that the asset allocation process accounts for 90% of a portfolio's performance over time. This means that less than 10% of the portfolio's performance depends upon fund managers and which individual securities they choose.

Joe's Knowledge and Assumptions

Joe, knowing very little about investing, decided he needed to educate himself. He read the literature that his employer provided, articles in business magazines and newspapers, and the funds' sales material.

Believing that history repeats itself, Joe wanted to know the track record of the five funds (money market, high-grade bond, stock, balanced, and a GIC) that his plan offered. Since the funds were all relatively new, however, he decided he could get a better picture of their possible performances by studying the track record of their underlying assets (stocks, bonds, cash).

To get this insight, Joe constructed Charts 23 and 24 using information gathered from reference books at the local library. In these charts, he grouped annual returns in 5% ranges and counted how many times an asset class's annual return fell within each range.

Joe approximated a balanced fund by assuming it consisted of 50% S&P 500 stocks and 50% Treasury notes. He was then able to calculate annual returns.

From his readings, Joe also assumed that the returns of the GIC account will be slightly higher than the coupon rate of five year Treasury notes.

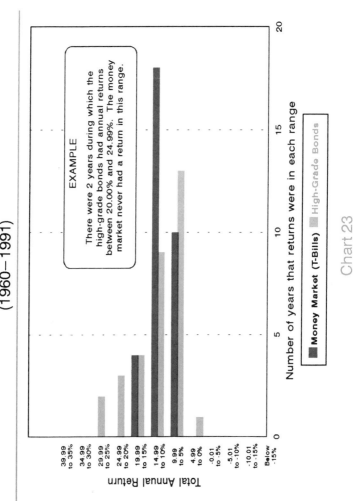

Past Performance of Money Market (T–Bills) and High–Grade Bonds
(1960–1991)

EXAMPLE

There were 2 years during which the high-grade bonds had annual returns between 20.00% and 24.99%. The money market never had a return in this range.

Total Annual Return

39.99 to 35%
34.99 to 30%
29.99 to 25%
24.99 to 20%
19.99 to 15%
14.99 to 10%
9.99 to 5%
4.99 to 0%
-0.01 to -5%
-5.01 to -10%
-10.01 to -15%
Below -15%

Number of years that returns were in each range

0   5   10   15   20

■ Money Market (T-Bills)   ▨ High-Grade Bonds

Chart 23

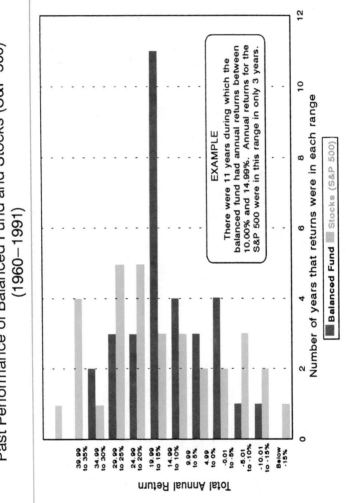

Past Performance of Balanced Fund and Stocks (S&P 500) (1960–1991)

Number of years that returns were in each range

Total Annual Return

39.99 to 35%
34.99 to 30%
29.99 to 25%
24.99 to 20%
19.99 to 15%
14.99 to 10%
9.99 to 5%
4.99 to 0%
-.01 to -5%
-5.01 to -10%
-10.01 to -15%
Below -15%

EXAMPLE

There were 11 years during which the balanced fund had annual returns between 10.00% and 14.99%. Annual returns for the S&P 500 were in this range in only 3 years.

■ Balanced Fund   ■ Stocks (S&P 500)

Chart 24

In What Assets Should Joe Invest?

Although stocks are extremely risky in the short-term, Joe learned that they are not all that risky over the long haul. (See Chart 5 in Chapter 2.) In fact, stocks have been the best performing assets over the long run. (See Chart 11 in Chapter 4.) Chart 24 also showed that stocks lost money in only eight out of the last 32 years. Moreover, they lost more than 15% in only one of the 32 years while they earned over 15% in sixteen of those years. Joe therefore feels that most of his money should go into stocks.

Since he might need some money before retirement, Joe wants the rest of his savings to get a more stable return. While he likes bonds, he worries about their market value fluctuations and how they reduce total return. (Chart 8 in Chapter 3 shows how changes in interest rates affect the prices, and thus total return, of bonds.) For example, in fourteen of the years studied, they had a total return of less than 5%. The returns of money market funds, however, fluctuate very little. These funds involve very little risk because they hold short-term investments like T-bills.

Joe has also learned that the insurance company which offers the GIC fund is financially sound. The fact that GICs are valued at book value (the amount invested plus previously earned interest) appeals to him because it makes them a very stable investment. Furthermore, GIC funds usually have higher returns than money market funds.

Since safety of principal is more important than high returns in his non-stock investments, Joe decides he should consider investing in either or both of the GIC and money market funds.

How Much Should Joe Invest in Each Type of Asset?

Joe was tempted to let the professionals answer this question by investing all of his money in the balanced fund. After reading the prospectus and talking to the fund's representative, however, Joe decides that it is not aggressive enough (i.e., not enough money goes into stocks).

Additionally, balanced fund managers use some form of market timing to shift their assets, and Joe has no faith in market timing. For the next 15 years or so, he wants a constant portion of his investments to be in stocks. Joe feels that it's not timing the market but how long you are in the market that counts. Thus, he rules out the balanced fund and puts 70% of his money into the stock fund.

Joe wants the rest of his account to have stable returns. However, if interest rates ever shoot up again, he might want to shift some money into bonds so that when interest rates fall, he can make a profit as the bonds increase in value. (Yes, Joe thinks he might be able to time the bond market.)

Joe knows that some GICs allow investors to get their money whenever they want, while others impose restrictions. He decides that, if the GIC in his plan allows him unlimited access to his money, he will put all 30% there. If not, he will put 15% in the GIC fund and 15% in the money market account.

How Should Joe Maintain His Asset Allocations?

Joe decides that once a year he will review his accounts and shift his assets to maintain the desired allocations (70% stock and 30% fixed-income). If his stock investments grow to over 70% of his total investments, he will sell some stock, lock in his profits, and reinvest the proceeds in fixed-income investments. If they fall below 70%, he will move some money from his fixed-income investments into stocks. Joe understands that you make money in the stock market by buying low and selling high, and this is what he plans on doing.

(If you have already accumulated sizeable amounts of money in your plan and feel that a major reallocation is needed, it might be wise to do it in installments over six months. However, asset shifts that result from annual reviews should be done at one time.)

Joe also realizes that, as retirement nears, he will have less time to recoup any stock market losses. Thus, he plans to gradually reduce his stock holdings beginning ten to twelve years before retirement. He wants, however, to leave enough money in the stock market to keep pace with inflation and capitalize on bull markets. At the same time, he will have enough money in fixed-income investments to protect himself against bear markets.